Original title:
Island Retreat

Copyright © 2025 Creative Arts Management OÜ
All rights reserved.

Author: Penelope Hawthorne
ISBN HARDBACK: 978-1-80581-633-1
ISBN PAPERBACK: 978-1-80581-160-2
ISBN EBOOK: 978-1-80581-633-1

Daydreaming by the Sea

Seagulls squawk as I sculpt in the sand,
A bucket and shovel, my dreams unplanned.
A crab walks by, it pinches my toe,
I chase it away, then yell out, "Whoa!"

Sunburned shoulders, I glance at my watch,
Time's slipping by, and I'm in a botch.
Ice cream drips down my brand-new shirt,
I laugh as it stains—life's happy dessert.

The waves do a dance, a splashy ballet,
A beach ball flies, then drifts far away.
I toss back my drink, and it spills on my knee,
Each sip's a reminder; it's just not for me!

As shadows grow long, and I search for my hat,
A dolphin pops up, "Well, how about that?"
We wave from the shore; they dive, oh so spry,
While I sit and munch on a slice of pie!

Enchanted Lagoon

In a cove where mermaids splash,
The seagulls dance and dolphins dash.
I'll take a nap on a rubber raft,
Dreaming of snacks, and a sandcastles' craft.

My drink is pink with umbrellas small,
While crabs host parties, they have a ball.
With flavors strong from a picnic spread,
Let's hope the ants don't plan instead!

Sails that Speak of Stillness

The boat sits still like a sleepy cat,
Waiting for wind, it's a lazy brat.
With sails flapping like a curtain's might,
We debate if lunch is better than flight.

A gull steals fries, the cheeky thief,
While we end up with a potato leaf.
The ocean's cozy, our laughs set free,
Until the tides toss us like a tea!

Moonlit Reflections

The moon's a pancake, tossed so high,
It lights the waves in a buttery sky.
With fireflies dancing like tiny stars,
We vow to catch one, but lose our jars.

The midnight snacks are crispy treats,
As we wade in waters, it tickles our feets.
A fish does a flip, and we all cheer,
Until we realize it just wants a beer!

The Beachcomber's Muse

With sandals squawking, I make my way,
Collecting seashells, what a fun play!
A jellyfish whispers, 'Catch me if you dare,'
While my towel dances in the salty air.

I stumble upon a grand old shoe,
What secrets it holds, if only it knew.
But no time for pondering, I must run fast,
Before it dawns on me, I've missed my last blast!

Solitude Beneath the Palms

Beneath the palms, I laid so still,
A crab walked by, it gave a thrill.
I tossed a chip, oh what a sight,
It grabbed my snack and took to flight!

The breeze it whispered, 'Take a break!'
I blinked and missed my sunburned fate.
A parrot squawked, 'What happened there?'
Now I look like a lobster, beware!

Echoes of Gentle Waves

Waves that crash with silly glee,
They splash and laugh, just like me.
A fish jumped out, a real high dive,
It flopped back down, looked disinclined!

With tousled hair and sandy toes,
I strutted past, striking poses.
But oh, the tide had plans in store,
It pulled me in, oh, what a chore!

Nestled in Tranquility

In a hammock, I tried to nap,
But all I got was a seagull's flap.
His beak was sharp, he stole my fries,
I shrieked aloud, 'Oh, sweet surprise!'

The sun was bright, the drinks were cold,
I claimed my spot, feeling bold.
Then a beach ball hit me with a thud,
Turns out, it was pure beachy crud!

Palm Trees and Starry Skies

At night, the palms swayed like a dance,
I joined in too, took my chance.
A coconut fell with a dull thump,
I ducked and rolled, good thing I'm spry!

The stars above, they twinkled bright,
I swirled around, what a kitesurf flight!
Then I tripped on my own two feet,
And laughed aloud, a funny feat!

Haven by the Sea

Seagulls squawk, a loud surprise,
Sunbathers snooze with sleepy sighs.
A crab on the sand, wears a tiny hat,
While a dog plays fetch with a flat old mat.

Ice cream drips, a sticky mess,
Laughter erupts, what a hot press!
Flip-flops squeak on the boardwalk floor,
Someone asks, 'Did I leave my keys on the shore?'

Driftwood Dreams

Driftwood castles by the waves,
Built by kids who like to rave.
A mermaid's tail, a wash of dreams,
Made from old t-shirts, or so it seems.

Jellyfish dance in the shallow tide,
While surfers wipe out, with no place to hide.
Pineapple hats, fruit cocktails in hand,
Complaining about how they should have planned.

Reflections in the Surf

The sun reflects on the bouncing waves,
While tourists in shorts look like knaves.
Sunburnt noses, melting ice cubes,
Trying to dance to the sea breeze grooves.

A dolphin jumps—a splash and swoosh,
But the seagulls dive for a French fry push.
Footprints flee from an incoming tide,
Leaving behind a shoe's weird slide.

A Sanctuary of Sand

Sandcastles crumbling by a rogue tide,
As a toddler approaches, full of pride.
His bucket's now home to a shrimp or two,
Mom's yelling loudly, 'Not food, boo-hoo!'

Beach towels tangled in a tight embrace,
As a seagull steals lunch, it's a race!
Flip-flop fights, let the laughter flow,
In this goofy, sandy, sun-drenched show.

Shores of Contemplation

Seagulls squawk, wearing shades,
Beach chairs stand in sun parades.
A crab breaks dance upon the sand,
While tourists wield ice cream in hand.

Flip-flops flop with comic grace,
Sunscreen blobs all over the place.
A seagull snatches someone's fry,
While laughter rings under the sky.

Between Ocean and Sky

Tommy tried to catch the breeze,
Instead, he tripped on his own knees.
Kites tangled in a palm tree's grasp,
While a sunburned dad took a gasp.

Waves crash down with a splashy roar,
As kids scream, begging for more.
Sandy sandwiches filled with grit,
Ranked as the best beach picnic hit!

Waterside Reverie

Seashells whisper secrets loud,
While mom sunbathes, feeling proud.
Dad's fishing pole gets tangled tight,
Hooking a shoe instead of a bite.

The tide rolls in with a goofy grin,
A sunburn frown reveals his skin.
Floating toys shaped like a whale,
In a race that's destined to fail!

Serenity in Every Grain of Sand

Flip-flop fashion helps us shine,
But lost the left one every time.
A treasure map drawn in sunscreen,
Leads to a spot where dreams are seen.

Yoga poses with sand-filled toes,
While a loud party next door grows.
Ocean waves call with silly tones,
As laughter dances among the bones.

Moonlit Escape

Under the stars, we dance quite weird,
The sand's our stage, oh how we cheered.
With a crab as our friend, pinching our toes,
We twirled and stumbled, striking a pose.

A coconut falls, gives us a fright,
Is it fate or just poor aim tonight?
We laugh till we snort, what a lovely sight,
In this whimsical hour, all feels just right.

Lullabies of the Lagoon

The frogs serenade with a ribbit or two,
While fishes join in, giving a view.
We float on our backs, gazing up high,
Giggling like kids, as clouds drift by.

A turtle glides past, with a curious stare,
"Join the party!" we shout, "Don't you dare glare!"
He shrugs his small shoulders, just wants to munch,
We offer him snacks; he's not here for punch.

Waves of Whispering Calm

The ocean whispers jokes, soft and light,
Promises of mischief by morning's first light.
We ride on the waves, like pros gone wrong,
Falling and laughing, our bellies all strong.

A seagull swoops down, stealing our fries,
With a cheeky squawk, right before our eyes.
We chortle and chase, it's a food battle game,
Who knew beach time could be so insane?

The Canvas of Seagulls

Seagulls are artists, with talent, it seems,
Painting the sky with their raucous screams.
They dive through the air, like clowns in a show,
Using our sandwiches as props for their flow.

With each gust of wind, our hats take flight,
Chasing them down feels absurdly right.
Laughter erupts as we stumble and trip,
In this circus of gulls, we're part of the script.

Vibrations of the Horizon

The seagulls squawk, they're quite the crew,
Dancing in circles, as if they knew.
Sandy toes wiggle with laughter so sweet,
Crabs in the mix think they're hard to beat.

Sunburned tourists with hats too wide,
Slip on their flip-flops, ready to glide.
Beach balls collide in a colorful spree,
As someone shouts, "Hey, don't sit on me!"

Tanned folks argue about the best tan,
While seagulls plot how to steal their ham.
A beach chair race, which one will win?
Spoiler alert: it's the one with gin!

Ice cream melts faster than they can lick,
Spilling on shirts, oh, what a trick!
Joyful chaos, a sight to behold,
Beach life's a circus, and it never gets old.

Twilight on the Shore

As the sunset spills like spilled paint,
Crabs form a band, but they can't quite sync.
A conch shell rings like a call to arms,
Fishermen search for their lost lucky charms.

Laughter echoes as flip-flops flop,
The beach ball bounces, never will stop.
Kids chase the waves, a slippery race,
While a brave dog attempts the high dive space!

Sandcastles stand proud with flags in the breeze,
But watch out for waves, they might need a freeze.
Sandy-haired children, no worries today,
Except where the snacks have all gone astray!

Fishermen's tales grow taller each night,
"Caught a fish this big!" What a sight!
Twilight whispers secrets, it's time to unwind,
As the moon takes the stage, ever so kind.

Solstice Serenity

On the longest day, we feast just right,
With burgers and jokes flying in flight.
A watermelon slice drops, oh what a mess,
"It's cardio now!" someone yells in distress.

The sun's up high, it's a sizzle and bake,
Rubber ducky races, make no mistake!
Inflatables bob like jelly in glee,
While sunscreen battles are a sight to see.

A hammock sways with friendship's good cheer,
As someone yells, "Hey, is that a beer?"
Coconut drinks with umbrellas so bright,
Cheers to the laughter that fills up the night!

As day turns to twilight, and stars start to twinkle,
Someone's snoring loudly, can't even thinkle.
It's blissful chaos, this calorie spree,
In the warmth of the sun, just you and me.

Sun-Kissed Getaway

Sunglasses on, we're feeling so cool,
Sipping our drinks by the shimmering pool.
In the distance, the barbie starts to hum,
While someone insists, "I'm definitely fun!"

Hot dogs and laughter, a feast for the clan,
A beach party's missing a grooving plan.
Someone breaks out the dad dance reveal,
As kids throw beach balls with zest and zeal.

Sand tousled hair tells tales of the unkempt,
While the seagulls squawk as if they'd exempt.
Catch me a wave, says a brave little chap,
"Oops, never mind—I just fell in a lap!"

Under stars, the night comes alive,
With ghost stories shared, we scrunch and we jive.
Who knew vacations would end in a spree?
From sun-kissed mornings to wild reverie!

Abode of Tranquil Thoughts

A hammock strung between two trees,
The only thing I hear is bees.
They buzz and hum, but oh dear me,
My drink just spilled, now it's a spree.

I chase the crabs, they scuttle fast,
They laugh at me; I'm not too vast.
They pinch my toes; it's quite the blast,
I'm stuck in sand—what a contrast!

The sun shines bright, my hat's a sail,
I find a fish; it tells a tale.
It jumped right out, I dropped my ale,
Guess I'll be having soda pale.

A seagull swoops, it's quite a show,
It steals my chips, I start to go.
Chasing it down, oh where'd it go?
Just me and gulls—this comedy flow.

Celestial Shoreline

The waves come in; they sneak your chair,
It disappears—a prankster's affair.
I shout and laugh, with salty hair,
As flip-flops fly through summer air.

A beach ball rolls to someone's feet,
They kick it back; oh what a treat!
But then it lands on my sun-bleached seat,
And bounces me back—such a feat!

The sun's so hot, I grab my shade,
But it flies off; oh what a raid!
Chasing it down, I've been dismayed,
Who knew my fun would get delayed?

So now I lounge with squawking friends,
Trading tall tales that never ends.
Under the sun, my laughter bends,
As silly moments, the daylight lends.

Whimsy in the Wind

Kites in the air, all colors and cheer,
They dance and dip, quite far but near.
I trip on my shoelace—oh dear!
The wind's a joker, let's make it clear.

A crab on the shore with a funny grin,
Small as my thumb, yet full of vim.
He pinches my toe, it makes me spin,
Then scuttles away; how rude of him!

The salty breeze carries laughter loud,
A seagull joins and feels so proud.
I share my sandwich with the crowd,
Turns out it's them who are quite avowed.

As sunset glows, I watch them play,
A merry band at close of day.
Their antics set my cares away,
With a wink and laugh, I've won the fray.

Shores of Timelessness

A towel castle, kids dig with glee,
While I sip drinks beneath a tree.
The waves crash down, but what's that we see?
My sun hat floats, oh silly me!

Some pelicans dive, making waves splash,
They steal my snacks in a quick dash.
I yell in jest, they make a splash,
My picnic's gone; it's quite the clash!

The tide rolls in with a gentle sigh,
Footprints washed away where dreams lie.
I chase the tide as moon climbs high,
Giggling like a kid, oh my, oh my!

As dusk falls soft with wrinkled lines,
I sit and smile at tales and signs.
With salty lips and clinking wines,
I wrap my day in goofy shrines.

A Breath of Salty Air

Waves crash and splatter, quite the show,
As seagulls squawk, stealing my fries,
My sunhat flies off in the brisk blow,
Chasing it down, oh what a surprise!

A crab tried to pinch my sandwich near,
I think it prefers crusty bread,
Laughter erupts; my friends all cheer,
While I dodge the crustacean and dread.

The sunburn's creeping, red like a clown,
I'm a lobster caught out on a spree,
But sea breeze whispers, 'Don't wear a frown!'
So here I am, sipping my tea!

Salty air fills my nose with glee,
As flip-flops flounder in the sand,
Each misstep makes a great comedy,
And I think I'll take a stand!

Nature's Embrace

Butterflies dance, and so do I,
A shimmy, a shake on nature's floor,
A bee buzzed by, quite bold and spry,
As I ducked, oh man, is that a chore!

Trees whisper secrets of the great unknown,
I'm convinced they gossip and share,
With roots underground, they're not alone,
I wonder if they laugh at my hair!

There's a parrot nearby that squawks so loud,
I think it's mocking my fancy hat,
With colors bright, my head feels proud,
Until it steals it! Now how about that?

Nature gives hugs, though some are sticky,
Like that mud puddle I just leapt through,
My flip was epic, but oh so tricky,
Now I'm covered! Who knew it was goo!

Lagoon's Lull

In calm waters, I paddle with flair,
A big splash sends the fish away,
My friends laugh hard, 'You're quite the bear!'
They forgot their boat and guess who's stay?

A turtle pokes its head in surprise,
Did I just scare off the local crew?
With eyes so wide, I realize,
That splash made my worries feel anew.

I attempted a pose, hoping for grace,
But instead, I slipped and fell in quick,
The lagoon giggles; it's quite the place,
As I emerge feeling cold and slick!

The sunset glows, painting the sky,
But I'm the star of this watery show,
With laughter and warmth, I can't deny,
In my soggy gear, I steal the glow!

Hideaway Haven

In a cozy nook, I sip my drink,
With an umbrella perched on the rim,
I wave to the locals, they start to wink,
While I contemplate my sandy whim.

A lizard joins me, uninvited at best,
As I munch on snacks and enjoy the scene,
It eyes my chips like a crafty jest,
I must protect my salty cuisine!

The hammock sways; I catch a nap,
Only to wake with drool on my chin,
I thought I was still caught in a trap,
But it's just the afternoon's lazy spin.

Laughing at life, as the tide rolls in,
I tumble and giggle, it's all just play,
In my hideaway, where troubles are thin,
I'll dance with the breeze, come what may!

Calming Currents of the Heart

Waves tickle toes in the sand,
Seagulls squawk, as if they've planned.
My drink's umbrella's blown away,
"That's fine," I say, "It's a sunny day!"

Friends in hammocks sing off-key,
Lost in laughter, wild and free.
A crab scuttles by, gives me a stare,
"Hey buddy, don't you have a shell to wear?"

Tropic drinks slip from my hand,
They splatter all over the land.
"Oops!" I cry as folks just cheer,
In this paradise, there's nothing to fear!

Sunburned noses, giggles abound,
We dance to the waves' silly sound.
With every splash, our cares are tossed,
Here's to fun, never lost!

The Last Echo of the Sunset

The sun dips low, a cheeky wink,
"Stay but a moment," it starts to think.
We gather 'round with snacks galore,
A race for munchies from the shore!

The sky's on fire, like a pie misplaced,
Everyone laughs with sun-kissed face.
"I'm no Picasso," says my friend,
"Just an artist with snacks to lend!"

As night creeps in, bugs start to whine,
"I think they like our Groupon wine!"
Someone yelps as a critter lands,
We're swatting at air with our flailing hands.

Amidst the giggles and slight dismay,
The stars come out, sending troubles away.
"We'll toast to this, with a chocolate bar!"
Life's sweetest moments, bizarre yet bizarre!

A Touch of the Tropics

In flip-flops, I stumble and sway,
Trying to dance, but it's more like play.
The rhythm's strong, but I'm missing a beat,
Though coconuts roll, I'm on my feet!

A parrot squawks, "You call that a move?"
I laugh, grab a fish, and start to groove.
The locals join, with a wink and a cheer,
"Let's make some waves, and avoid the beer!"

With cocktails in hand, we all toast loud,
To the silliest moments, a goofy crowd.
Belly flops echo, as laughter spills,
In this tropical haze, we cure our ills.

When night falls, our fun won't cease,
As we hiccup out jokes, feeling quite at peace.
"Life's just a party, don't take it in stride,"
Here's to laughter and fun, come join the ride!

Meditations by the Thundering Surf

The waves roll in with a booming roar,
I sit on the shore, but I watch my score.
"Zen is easy," my buddy yells out,
"Just meditate between bites of trout!"

The surf swells up, big enough to splash,
I signal a whale, but I just made a crash.
With seaweed hats, we giggle away,
"Nature's styling!" we both proclaim!

As the tide comes in, my shoes float away,
"Meditation strong," I cry in dismay.
We chase the sea, like dogs on a spree,
Finding treasures like shells, oh look! That's free!

With chants and an odd crab dance in tow,
We laugh so much our worries just go.
"The ocean's our stage, we're stars, you see?"
This wacky retreat feels just like family!

Vibrant Sunset Soliloquy

The sun plops down like a big yellow fruit,
It splashes the sky, oh what a hoot!
Seagulls squawk while sipping on fizz,
I wave back, hoping they understand my whiz.

Flip-flops flapping, I dance with glee,
A crab joins in, what a sight to see!
Pineapple drinks spill from hand to face,
Each sip a giggle, each laugh a chase.

Tides tickle toes in a playful embrace,
Sandcastles crumble, but I won't leave a trace.
A sunset selfie? Oh, strike a pose,
With a goofy grin, the laughter flows.

As night draws near, stars start to wink,
In this paradise, stress starts to sink.
Gazing up, I feel such bliss,
Life's simple joys, I just can't miss.

Journey to Stillness

With a suitcase packed with snacks galore,
I land on a shore, craving more and more.
The palms wave hi, they're dressed so fine,
I trip over a flip-flop, oh how divine!

A hammock sways like a lazy cat,
Got stuck inside it, imagine that!
The book I dropped, now a clever kite,
The breeze says hi, as I squeal with delight.

Here the clocks tick backward, time takes a break,
Nothing to do, except frolic and shake.
I spot a coconut, so tempting to eat,
It rolls away—oh, what a feat!

Seagulls join in like they own the place,
I dance with a crab, what a funny race.
In this stillness, joy takes the lead,
In a comical world, we all take heed.

Enchanted Waterscape

The waves chuckle with a splash and roar,
As I dip my toes, wanting more and more.
A fish pops up, with a cheeky grin,
I wink back, let the funny times begin!

Snorkel gear on, I jump like a fool,
Swimming with turtles, breaking every rule.
They glide with grace, I wiggle instead,
The seaweed wraps—oh, what a thread!

Flippers flapping, I take a dive,
Bubbles rise up, it's fun to revive.
Mermaids giggle and wave from afar,
"Join us!" they call, "You'll be a star!"

But back on the shore, I start to leap,
Sand on my nose, oh, it's quite a heap.
With all the laughter, I look like a clown,
In this watery world, I won't ever frown.

Seafoam Symphony

A tune in the air, the waves' joyful beat,
The seafoam dances, it's light on its feet.
A conch shell sings, it's quite a sight,
I shimmy along, giving it all my might!

With seashells clattering, a musical buzz,
Every wave a note, just because.
I gather driftwood, make a fine band,
Playing tunes for jellyfish, isn't life grand?

The sand is my stage, under skies so blue,
Performing for crabs, with an audience crew.
Each flip and flop draws laughter and cheer,
Oh, how I wish every day could be here!

As dusk falls down, guitars in the sand,
With melodies rich, we form a grand band.
In the seafoam's lullaby, we find delight,
Singing silly songs 'til the stars shine bright.

Echoes of the Tranquil Shore

I woke up thinking I was the queen,
But the seagulls squawked, quite mean!
My crown is a bucket, bright and round,
And my throne? A beach chair—oh, so profound!

The waves are laughing, it's a real show,
I tried to surf, but fell, whoa-ho!
With sand in my shorts and dreams in my head,
I gracefully flopped, like a fish out of bed!

A picnic was planned with snacks so divine,
But seagulls attacked, said, "That's now all mine!"
I chased them away with a loud flail and yell,
Only to trip in a sandcastle—oh well!

So here's to the fun, the sun, and the more,
With laughter and blunders, who could ask for more?
Each wave brings a tale, a giggle or snort,
On this comical shore, life's a sandy sport!

Castaway's Haven

Castaway dreams on my makeshift throne,
A wooden plank to sit, I call my own.
Laying back, sipping coconut juice,
My smile's so wide, I might introduce!

The sun blazes down, making me melt,
Should have packed ice cream instead of felt!
Seals swim by, giving me the eye,
"Do you swim, human?" with a laugh and a sigh!

I tried to fish with a line made of grass,
But it's much harder to catch a splashy bass.
Instead, I snagged a flip-flop, oh dear,
The sole of my footwear just won't share cheer!

Sandy toes and a hat full of fun,
Under the palms, I shout, "I'm number one!"
With chuckles from crabs and whispers from breeze,
This castaway life is a laugh, if you please!

A Breath of Salty Air

Morning's here with salty delight,
I fumble my breakfast, what a sight!
As toast flies off, it dances in glee,
The gulls just laugh, "That's a meal for me!"

I step on the sand and trip on a shell,
"Goodbye!" goes my smoothie, it bids farewell.
The waves crash in, the tide takes my flip,
I dive for it quick—oh, what a slip!

Shells all around, like treasure unseen,
I wear them like jewels, oh so keen.
But each time I pose for my holiday pic,
One rolls away, what a sneaky trick!

As dusk settles in, I toast with my drink,
To the funny mishaps that make me rethink.
Here's to each wave, each stumble and scare,
With laughter aplenty, it's beyond compare!

Solace in the Sands

Beneath my umbrella, in shades of bright hue,
I sip on a drink, it's mostly just glue.
The ice that's supposed to keep it so chill,
Has melted away—oh, what a thrill!

The sunbathers nearby all snicker and smirk,
As I get up, pretending I'm a great perk.
A dance with the wind, I trip on my feet,
With laughter erupting, I can't take the heat!

I built a grand castle, with moats all around,
But the tide came in, and the waves did abound.
What once was a fortress is now just a mess,
With crabs on the loose, I can't help but confess!

So here in the sands, I find my retreat,
With giggles and hiccups, life's hard to beat.
Though sticky and sandy, my heart's full of cheer,
In this comical paradise, I can't help but steer!

Whispers of the Breeze

Gentle winds play with my hat,
It's dancing like a silly cat.
Palm trees laugh, they sway and bend,
I swear they're plotting with my friend.

Seagulls squawk like they own the place,
I think they're sporting quite a face.
Chasing crabs who scuttle away,
Their pinching jokes make my day.

Sipping drinks with a tiny umbrella,
I spill it all, what a fella!
Sun-kissed skin with a spritz of toast,
On this havana, I'm truly the host.

Sand between my toes makes me giggle,
As I stumble, I start to wiggle.
Here with laughter and no strife,
I've traded work for a silly life.

Harbor of Dreams

The boat rocks like it's lost its mind,
As I search for snacks I can't seem to find.
Fish jump around, having a bash,
While I nibble on chips, making a crash.

Captain's hat's too big for my head,
Against the wind, I'm barely led.
"Ahoy there!" I call to a passing seal,
He rolls his eyes—guess he's not real.

Waves are playing their jumpy games,
Making the boat twist with embarrassing names.
Splashing water, I slip and slide,
I'm the captain now—take me for a ride!

Even the sun is cracking a grin,
As I struggle to paddle with little win.
In this spot where chaos reigns,
I've discovered joy in all the pains.

Respite with the Waves

Waves crash like they're in a race,
I flop on the sand, it's a sunny place.
Shells whisper secrets, soft and sweet,
While I trip over, oh, my poor feet!

With sunglasses that are way too bright,
I misjudged the morning light.
Burnt to a crisp, now I'm a lobster,
Complaining to crabs, "You're a monster!"

Ice cream drips down the cone I clutch,
I laugh and moan—this is too much!
Every bite's a sticky affair,
But with laughter, I'll hide my despair.

Beach balls bounce like they've lost their way,
As friends throw them into my face today.
In this silly swirl of sun and fun,
I'm learning life's best when it's done on the run.

Retreat of the Heart

Laughter echoes within my chest,
Here's to the fun; I'm truly blessed.
Hammocks sway like they've lost their chill,
I'm a giggling blob, what a thrill!

Sunburned noses, what a sight,
We look like tomatoes in the sunlight.
Playing games like we're still in school,
Splashing around like we're all fools.

Picnics spread with a generous hand,
Finding ants who dream of a grand band.
As we munch on sandwiches that fall apart,
The crumbs are confetti for this wild heart.

At dusk, we gather to share our tales,
With giggles that float like delicate sails.
This joyful place had captured my soul,
In the retreat of fun, I've found my whole.

Cascade of Colors

Amidst the hues of bright delight,
Lemonade laughs on a summer night.
A parrot dances, thinking it's sly,
While we try to catch a coconut pie.

Flip-flops fly, oh what a sight,
As kids chase crabs, with great delight.
A rainbow splash, a splash of fun,
Splash-tastic moments, oh where's my bun?

Kite tails tangle in the beach breeze,
Sandy surprises hide with such ease.
The sun sets low, the colors merge,
As we miscount seagulls on the verge.

What a scatter of bright escape,
Funny faces in the sea shape.
In the laughter, we all unite,
In every wave, we find our light.

Shelter of Seclusion

In a hammock made of yarn and dreams,
A squirrel steals snacks, or so it seems.
Tropical fruit has taken its toll,
Banana peels threaten my stroll.

Napping iguanas think they own this place,
While I play hide and seek with my face.
Palm trees wave, with sarcastic flair,
As I fumble snacks caught in my hair.

Sippin' coconuts, feeling so bold,
The weather's a joke; it's sweltering cold.
I sip my drink, and it slips away,
Just watch it float, oh what a play!

Seclusion here has quite the effect,
Laughter echoes, perfect to select.
With every giggle, we start to groove,
In this quiet chaos, we find our move.

Basking in Warmth

Sunkissed tan and sunglasses cool,
I made a sandcastle; it's now a pool.
Seagulls squawk, thinking they're grand,
While I try to toss shells, just using my hand.

A beach ball bounces, what a delight,
Trying to catch it? It's quite a sight.
With each little giggle, the waves respond,
As I trip on a towel; my grace is gone.

With ice cream melting down my chin,
I yell for help; the battle begins!
A curious crab might just join the fray,
As I dance with laughter, I just want to play.

Under the sun, with humor so bright,
Each moment's a giggle, each sunset a sight.
In the warmth of the day, we all convene,
Living life loudly, like a sea serine.

Ocean's Gentle Caress

The ocean whispers with a playful grin,
As I try paddleboarding, what a spin!
Falling flat, I make quite the splash,
And laughing dolphins seem to make a dash.

A beach towel fights with the gusts of air,
Like a dancer caught in a wild affair.
Sandy snacks sneak past my eager hands,
While crabs critique our odd beach bands.

A shell collection, colorful and neat,
But every piece feels like a little cheat.
They snap back laughter, as I stand tall,
Only to trip—you guessed it, I fall!

With every wave, spirits seem to soar,
The jest of the sea keeps us wanting more.
In this gentle dance between sand and tide,
Humor and joy are forever our guide.

Drift Away

With drinks in hand, we start to sway,
Tropical tunes lead us astray.
A seagull steals my sandwich snack,
I yell at him, he squawks right back!

The sun is blazing, oh what a scene,
I'm melting faster than ice cream!
A crab in shades walks by with flair,
Does he know he's quite the scare?

Harmonies of the Horizon

We gathered shells to make a band,
With ukuleles made of sand.
My friend forgot the chords to play,
But hey, who cares? It's another day!

The waves applaud our offbeat song,
It's completely right yet feels so wrong.
A dolphin leaps; we cheer, delight,
Turns out he sings better at night!

Footprints in the Sand

I walked alone, or so I thought,
My footprints show that I've been caught.
A crab stepped in to steal my trace,
  Do they have a stylish race?

A kid digs holes; we build, then fall,
I've got sand stuck in places small.
We laugh till waves wash all away,
  Tomorrow, we'll return to play!

Solitary Starlight

With stars above and snack to munch,
I sat alone, till I heard a crunch.
A raccoon joins, sneaky and sly,
I share my chips, but he looks high!

The moon gives me a cheeky grin,
That furry thief starts to spin.
While I'm poached out of my delight,
Next time, I'll hide my snack at night!

A Place Called Peace

In a hammock made for two,
I snooze and dream of stew.
The seagulls steal my chips,
While I drool and doze, not quite with grips.

Palm trees sway with grace,
As I try to find my place.
The sunburn's red, a gecko laughs,
Chasing shadows as the morning drafts.

My drink's got an umbrella, oh so bright,
But it's melting fast, what a sight!
I wave hello to passing boats,
They think I'm waving; I'm just on my floats.

With sand between my toes so fine,
I ponder if I need a sign.
"Don't feed the crabs, they steal your thing,"
But here they are, plotting with a fling.

Solitary Escape

I packed my bags for some alone,
Only to find the lizards have grown.
They dance and flip, and to my surprise,
One's wearing shades, oh, how he tries!

The coconut drinks are all I need,
Until the squirrels steal my full speed.
I chase them down, a silly sight,
Two squirrels with my snack, they take flight!

No Wi-Fi here, just me and the sea,
Talking to shells, they talk back, whee!
The crabs are my companions, oh what fun,
But they pinch too much; I'd better run.

I'll have to dig for some fresh meat,
But all I find are crabby feet.
As I sit here on this rock with glee,
Oh, bring on the lizards; we'll form a spree!

Under the Stars at Dusk

The evening sky begins to glow,
As I trip on sand and stub my toe.
Stars twinkle bright, a cosmic show,
But watch out! Here comes the tidal flow.

My perfect spot to watch the night,
Suddenly feels like a salmon flight.
The moon looks down with a knowing grin,
As I splash and giggle, let the fun begin!

A blanket spread, snacks all around,
But seagulls swoop in—what trouble I've found!
"Hey! That's my sandwich!" I call in vain,
They laugh and squawk, it's all in the game.

Under the stars, I make my plea,
"More snacks, less fuss!" says the open sea.
Moonbeams dance, crabs join the fun,
Tonight's a party, for everyone!

Tidal Reflections

With my toes in the tidal waves,
I ponder how life often behaves.
A crab scuttles by, with a wink and a nudge,
He's got sass for days, holds a grudge!

The sun's set low, the colors ignite,
Splashing waves, oh, what a sight!
I slip and slide, as the tide gives chase,
Trying to dance in this watery space.

Reflection in water, just like a play,
But the fish are judging, oh, what can I say?
"Keep it down, folks, I'm trying to shine!"
They giggle and splutter, "You're out of line!"

So here I am, at the edge of fun,
With a seagull's chorus, my own silly pun.
As the tides come in, I'll raise a cheer,
Funny fish tales, I'll hold dear!

Sunlit Solace

In shorts and flip-flops, I dance on the sand,
Trying to impress a sunbathing band.
Seagulls laugh loudly, they steal my snack,
I chase them in circles, but they don't hold back.

The sunflowers wobble, they lean for a drink,
As I sip my coconut and try not to think.
A crab in a tuxedo prances on by,
I ask, "Is that style?" He just rolls his eye.

My towel a fortress, my hat a great shield,
Deflecting the rays like a battle field.
A peek into the shade, a nap sounds just right,
Until I awaken with sand in my bite!

The ocean waves giggle, they tickle my toes,
A game of hide-and-seek with the tide, I suppose.
I dive into laughter, the waves they all play,
As I splash and I snicker the afternoon away.

Breezes of Bliss

With sunny delight, I sip lemonade,
My beach chair is cozy, my budget's been made.
I watch as my friend attempts to build high,
A sandcastle fortress that flops on the fly.

A gust of warm breezes, a friendly cow mooed,
I turn to the surf and it chuckles, not rude.
A kite in the sky does an accidental dive,
My soda now sits in the sand: hope it survives!

Palm trees are swaying, a tropical dance,
While I groove to the tunes of a conch shell's chance.
Then a wave gives a wink, splashes me with glee,
Did that sea just tease? Yes, it's mocking me!

Sunsets in colors that dazzle and cheer,
The ocean whispers secrets that only we hear.
I laugh with the stars, they wink back with flair,
In this silly paradise, there's joy in the air!

Coral Cradles

I donned my snorkel, took a dive with glee,
But my flippers flopped wildly, oh woe is me!
Fish giggle behind coral, a secretive lot,
As I splash and I flounder, they swim off to plot.

A sea turtle giggles, it glides past my face,
With an air of great wisdom, it floats in such grace.
I wave with my flipper, my gesture so grand,
But it shakes its wise head like "You don't understand."

Bright starfish applaud on the ocean bed floor,
As I struggle to float but just sink more and more.
A flamboyant starfish yells out, "What a sight!"
"Next time wear a life vest — it'll save you tonight!"

I wobble back up, to the sunlight I call,
With tales of my flops and my underwater fall.
The ocean stretched wide, with laughter its grace,
In this whimsical world, I'll embrace my place!

Hideaway of Heartbeats

In a hammock I'll swing, with a drink made of lime,
The bugs start a party, they dance out of time.
I swat at the critters, they buzz and they flee,
Yet they come back for dinner — rude company, whee!

A crab darts past me, it knows all the rules,
While I'm here looking like a jester to fools.
Underneath my sunglasses, I blink at the light,
"Will someone please tell me, is there fish in sight?"

A parrot squawks loudly, "You call this a nap?"
My heart races quickly, "This is my favorite trap!"
With feathers all glimmering, it narrates my fail,
I chuckle and grin, lost in this endless tale.

The moon casts a glow as I settle in tight,
With critters for company — what a silly night!
In the corner of laughter, all worries depart,
In this haven of giggles, I cradle my heart.

Silhouettes at Dusk

Palm trees dance like they're in a show,
While I trip over sand, oh no, not so!
Laughter erupts from a nearby shack,
As I spill my drink and my funny snack.

Seagulls squawk with sass in the air,
They mock my sunburn, but I don't care!
Flip-flops get stuck in the marshy floor,
And I question if I've walked here before.

When the sun dips low, we spin in glee,
In our goofy hats, it's quite a sight to see!
The night brings a dance, we twirl and slide,
On this sandy stage, we take our pride.

So as the stars wink and the mimosas flow,
I stumble on purpose, oh what a show!
With friends by my side and laughter galore,
This sunset haven, who could ask for more?

Breeze-Kissed Bliss

A light gust tickles my sun-soaked nose,
It lifts my hat, where it lands who knows?
Coconuts giggle from the palm tree tops,
As I chase my drinks, my balance just drops.

Flip-flops flapping like wings of a bird,
Each step I take is a slapstick word!
The breeze brings whispers that carry my laughs,
While I attempt yoga on swaying staffs.

Children giggle as I stumble along,
Trying to join in their cheerful song.
The swing set creaks with my elegant flair,
While I swing too high, "I'm flying!" I declare.

In this wavy oasis, I forget my woes,
With the breeze's tickle and soft, sandy toes.
A perfect day filled with giggles and bliss,
As I hug the palm tree, oh what a kiss!

Colorful Coral Gardens

Beneath the waves, the fish wear a frown,
As I splash in, looking like a clown!
Corals resemble candy, a feast for the eyes,
I grab my snorkel, ready for surprise.

Bubbles escape like giggles on cue,
While I chase starfish that dart straight through.
A crab in a tuxedo pretends to be grand,
I bow to him, oh what a neat hand!

Seaweed tickles, giving me a fright,
As I whirl and twirl, what a comical sight!
In a colorful world, I laugh with the squids,
Who join in my dance, they wriggle like kids.

Emerging above with a splash and a cheer,
I shake off the water, no worries here!
With vibrant hues filling the sun's golden rays,
I'm just a goofball, in this aquatic ballet!

The Oasis of Thought

In a hammock strung between two tall trees,
I ponder my snacks, and the last time I sneezed.
I reflect on my woes, confined in this space,
Like a crab dreaming of marathon race.

The breeze plays tricks, it tangles my hair,
I ponder if it's trying to be fair.
As the sun drips low, I sip on my drink,
Was it coconut water, or just a pink wink?

My thoughts drift and wander, as the ducks quack loud,
What's more precious, my nap or this crowd?
I see squirrels with acorns, plotting a feast,
While my brain's in limbo, I laugh like a beast.

In this retreat of thoughts, I let my mind float,
With giggles that bubble like a whimsical boat.
In the shade of the palms, I'll dream to absurd,
With laughter my guide, I'll fly like a bird!

Sanctuary of Solitude

A hammock hangs between two trees,
Where time itself will softly tease.
With squirrels as my entertainment chore,
I laugh at seagulls circling for more.

The sun's a wink, the breeze a grin,
In this place, tranquility begins.
I sip on coconut—what a delight,
While my flip-flops take off in flight!

A crab decides he's king today,
He scuttles off, claims his sway.
I try to dance, trip on my toes,
This area's wild—no one quite knows!

Even the pineapples wear shades with flair,
While dancing sunbeams tease my hair.
Should I build a sandcastle tall?
Or invite the fish for a poolside brawl?

Whispering Waves of Refuge

The waves come sipping from afar,
Like friendly neighbors at a bar.
They crash and giggle, splash and play,
Hope no one spills their drink today!

I brought a chair—what a mistake,
It blew away, now I must shake!
The fish are laughing, quite the jest,
They'll have a tale for all the rest!

A dolphin pokes his head to view,
With a flip and a twist, he bids adieu.
'Bring a snack next time!' he flashes a smile,
But I swear I'm witty—really worth a while!

Here's to sunburns and sandy toes,
And singing tunes that everyone knows.
Let's toast to the crabs, the gulls, and my hat,
As I tumble back into my sun-spray vat!

The Hidden Cove of Calm

Beneath a rock, a treasure lies,
Not gold, but snacks—what a surprise!
I munch on chips, such crunchy bliss,
While geckos dance, not wanting to miss.

The waves high-five as they roll ashore,
Each splash a giggle, begging for more.
My flip-flops float, the tide they steal,
Only to return with squeaky zeal!

A lobster claims he's missing the show,
While I just stare, struck by the flow.
I can't tell if I'm a guest or the host,
In this strange party with a seafood boast!

Coconut cups all round they cheer,
Even the seaweed joins to reappear.
I kick back, laugh, and let out a shout,
This hidden cove's what life's all about!

Serenity in the Sway of Palms

The palms sway to a silent tune,
Like awkward dancers under the moon.
A squirrel's jive makes everyone grin,
As I attempt to join, but lose my spin!

I found a hat—wonderful flair,
Now I'm just hoping no bird will dare.
The sand feels soft, a warm embrace,
Thanks to the tide, I've lost my place!

A pelican drops by, what a catch!
He's looking for food, so I shared a batch.
Together we cackle, what a funny pair,
I think he stole my last slice of pear!

As dusk falls with silly delight,
Fireflies twinkle, taking flight.
With laughter echoing 'neath the stars,
I'll remember this retreat, by the jars!

Solitary Footprints in the Sand

In the soft sand, I took a stroll,
My feet left marks, like a lost shoal.
A hermit crab waved, said, "Hey, don't flee!"
But I tripped over seaweed—oh, woe is me!

Seagulls squawked, a raucous choir,
They mocked my dance, oh, how they conspire!
With a crabby critter as my guide,
I attempted to moonwalk—what a wild ride!

Salty breeze tickled, made me giggle,
I tried to prance, but only did a wiggle.
The sun was setting, all colors gleamed,
While I face-planted, blissful and dreamed!

When evening comes, the footprints fade,
My laughter lingers where the fun was made.
Now I resign to my cozy cocoon,
With dreams of dancing beneath the moon!

Illumination at Twilight's Edge

As sun dipped low, lights started to glow,
Frogs in tuxedos began the show.
They croaked their tunes with glee and grace,
While I clapped hands, keeping up the pace.

Fireflies fluttered like tiny fairies,
Waving goodbye to my wild miseries.
I tripped on twigs; oh, what a sight!
Even the twilight chuckled in delight.

A squirrel burst through, wearing a crown,
Claimed he was king of the dusty town.
He challenged me to a humorous race,
I accepted, then fell, what a disgrace!

But as the stars unveiled their light,
We shared a laugh, what a silly night.
In this sweet chaos beneath the trees,
I found laughter, like a soft breeze.

The Harbor of Inner Peace

A beach ball bobbed in a calm bay,
With my buddy the seal, we danced all day.
He swam with flair, I tried to keep up,
But he laughed so hard, spitting water in my cup!

The sun cast shadows, a playful scene,
I lay on my towel, quite serene.
But a crab crawled near, with pinchers aglow,
Tried to steal my fries; oh, what a show!

An old turtle joined, slow yet proud,
Said, "Don't rush, friend, let's hang with the crowd."
We played charades with waves as props,
While a ship's captain shouted, "Hey, don't drop!"

As night unfurled its starry cape,
I bid farewell to all escape.
With crabs and turtles, the moon did tease,
I found my harbor in giggles and ease.

Nature's Gentle Caress

The palm trees waltzed in the warm breeze,
Their swaying dance brought me to my knees.
A coconut fell—what a clatter!
It rolled near my toes; oh, does it matter?

Bunnies hopped in a flower parade,
Turning blooms into confetti, oh, what a trade!
One cheeky chap stole my lunch with glee,
While I laughed at his hops, as funny as can be!

Butterflies giggled, chased by the wind,
While the clouds overhead turned into a grin.
Each beat of nature's whimsical play,
Pulled at my heartstrings; I felt so okay!

As twilight brewed, I waved goodbye,
With funny tales of the day gone by.
In nature's arms, I found sweet embrace,
And spent the night with a smile on my face!

Dappled Sunlight on Quiet Waters

The sun sneezed through the trees, so bright,
Just like my uncle's shirt, quite a sight!
Fish splashed, wearing sparkles and glee,
While I danced on the dock, quite carefree.

A rubber duck sailed by with a quack,
Winking at seagulls, they'd cut him some slack.
I tried to fish, but caught only a shoe,
With a message inside: "We miss you, it's true!"

A crab joined my tea party, indignant and sly,
Claiming the bisque was too warm for his eye.
We laughed as he danced, his claws all aglow,
Even the sun couldn't steal the show!

Eventually, I slipped, took a dive in the pool,
Spreading chaos, oh what a splashy fool!
But sun-dappled laughter turned my frown upside down,
In my half-drenched glory, I wore the best crown!

The Palm Frond's Lullaby

The palm fronds whispered soft, sweet tunes,
While I crafted hats out of old coconuts' loons.
A monkey in shades danced on by,
Stealing my beach snacks—oh my, oh my!

Sandy toes wiggled, laughter all around,
As I twirled like a wizard, grace unbound.
But the sea breeze teased with a playful wave,
And my hat flew away; liberation, I braved!

I tripped on a crab and landed with glee,
The palm fronds snickered, "Now that's comedy!"
With my hairy new friend, we started a band,
Crustacean beats were simply quite grand!

Beneath the swaying palms, the party will roll,
As laughter and sun merge deep in my soul.
With a coconut drum and a flip-flop guitar,
We'll be famous for tunes from near and afar!

Forgotten Shores of Peace

Where the beach towel is my throne,
And seagulls plot mischief, all on their own.
I sip from a coconut, pretending I'm wise,
While sand tickles my nose—what a surprise!

Old flip-flops float by, they know no bounds,
Wearing memories of our beachy sounds.
I glance at the horizon, a sunburned sales rep,
With a map made of crayon, oh what a step!

A hermit crab wearing my lost ring,
Teases me gently, thinks he's the king!
As waves roll ideas like jelly on toast,
I chuckle at clouds that look like a ghost.

Forgotten shores hold treasures galore,
Like random shells and a squeaky old door.
With laughter the secret to staying afloat,
I toss back my head, and I happily gloat!

Driftwood Dreams

I found driftwood and named it Tim,
A wise wooden sage, with quite the whim.
He told me of mermaids who lost their way,
Dreaming of karaoke, night and day!

As I laid back, Tim humbly advised,
"Put your sunscreen on before you get fried!"
I laughed so hard that the sand leapt up,
Trying to sneak in my lemonade cup.

A crab with a monocle issued me a dare,
To dance with the gulls in the salty sea air.
With wings flapping wildly, and no sense of beat,
We pranced through the surf, oh what a treat!

As the sun began setting, a glorious sight,
Tim winked and said, "This feels just right!"
With laughter my anchor, and driftwood my dream,
I'd float through this life, or so it would seem!

Fluttering Hammock Dreams

In a hammock suspended high,
I see coconuts fall from the sky.
Like a piñata that's way too sly,
I just hope they're ripe and not dry.

The breeze whispers secrets to me,
About fish that fly like a bee.
I'll be sipping on sweet iced tea,
As a crab plays the ukulele with glee.

Seagulls argue, who knows what about,
Maybe they're in a feathered bout.
Meanwhile, I'm trying to shout,
To the waves, 'Turn that music out!'

And as the sun sets, hues on parade,
I wonder, why did I pick this trade?
Count me out of all the charade,
Just give me my snack and my shade.

Beneath the Coconut Canopy

Underneath the swaying trees,
I spot a crab that's hard to please.
He pinches my toe, 'Hey, that's not cheese!'
I jump and spill my drink with ease.

The parrots are gossiping loud,
About the weird things they've found.
One stole my sandwich, oh, I'm cowed,
But a laughing dolphin joins the crowd.

The sun shines bright, like a showoff,
As I try to shake sand from my loaf.
Why does my swimsuit feel so doff?
I'm convinced this was not my scoff.

With friends who are silly and wild,
We prance like each is a child.
In this world, I'm the most beguiled,
Forever chasing laughter, so styled.

Timeless Tides

The waves crash in a rhythmic beat,
Covered in sunscreen, I feel the heat.
A lighthouse dancer on my feet,
I attempt NOT to lose my seat!

The crabs are marching in formation,
Plotting a grand crustacean vacation.
They need a solid foundation,
For their dance-off celebration.

I try to build a sandcastle tall,
But it leans over like it's in a brawl.
Seagulls swoop down, making the call,
"Who invited that sand-blocking wall?"

As night falls, the stars take stance,
I think they're critiquing my dance.
The waves whisper, "Take a chance,"
And I stumble, I'm caught in a trance.

Serene Escape

On this beach, I've got my flair,
With flip-flops flying, no time to spare.
Seagulls plotting, a feathery pair,
While sunscreen's smeared all in my hair.

The surfboards line up for a race,
My dog's the winner, just in case.
He rides the waves with silly grace,
But looks concerned, who's made this place?

The hammock swings with a creaky sound,
In a sunlit world where fun is found.
Here, happiness is tightly wound,
Like my attempts at the limbo mound.

As laughter echoes, the sun starts dips,
I giggle with each wave that trips,
A vacation where joy tugs at our grips,
And the only regret is swimsuit slips.

Tranquility Found

I tried to sunbathe, oh what a sight,
But the seagulls found me, what a fright!
My sandwich vanished, oh such a crime,
Now I'm left with crumbs and a lime.

The beach ball bounced, it flew so high,
Hit a sunbather, I won't deny.
He jumped up shouting, 'That's not my game!'
I laughed so hard, I felt some shame.

A jellyfish passed by, with a gentle sway,
I swear it waved at me, in a funny way.
I thought it was friendly, so I waved back,
Turns out those tentacles went for my snack!

So here I sit with my drink in hand,
Cheers to the summer, oh isn't it grand?
Life's just a beach, with waves and a tan,
I'll take my laughter as far as I can.

Currents of Contentment

The boat tipped over, what a splash,
We landed in water, oh what a crash!
With laughter bubbling, we swam like dogs,
Chasing our cooler, it wobbled like frogs.

A crab made a move, I thought he would bite,
I ran in a circle, a comical sight.
"I just wanted snacks!" it seemed to say,
But I shrugged it off and danced far away.

The waves were so funny, shifting like cheese,
Caught a glimpse of a dolphin, oh, please!
He leapt and he flipped, like he was in a show,
I cheered for his stunts, he took quite a bow.

With sun on our backs and toes in the sand,
We laughed at our blunders, life was so grand.
In this watery world, bliss like a breeze,
A floaty in sight, with snacks—put me at ease.

Whispers of the Tides

The waves told secrets, like gossipy friends,
About sunburned tourists and their fashion trends.
I wore a big hat, like a queen on a spree,
While my sunglasses slid down, just to be free.

A crab 'crashed' my picnic, in style so divine,
He wore little shades, think he's feeling fine.
I offered him chips; he pinched my toe,
This beach life's wild, just thought you should know.

As footprints migrated, I lost my way,
Chasing a ball that had slipped from the bay.
I tripped on a flip-flop, oh what a scene,
Now I'm a legend, or so it would seem.

With laughter echoing, the sun setting low,
We danced on the shore, in our funny show.
Salt in our hair, and smiles so wide,
Tomorrow we'll surf, with the tides as our guide.

Serenity's Shore

I set up my towel, oh what a delight,
But a wave came charging, a humorous fright!
My stuff floated off, like a boat full of dreams,
Chased by a seagull, or so it seems.

The sandcastle I built, was a work of art,
Till a rogue wave understood my part.
It knocked it all down, like a sneeze in a crowd,
I scoffed at the ocean, oh, isn't it loud?

I spotted a crab with a daring little dance,
Was he showing off? Or just taking a chance?
I clapped and I cheered, like a fan in a pitch,
But forgot where I sat, now I'm in a ditch!

With sunscreen in hand, I'll try one more time,
To conquer this beach with my own rhythm rhyme.
As the sun starts to set with a fiery glow,
I'll treasure my laughter, and let it all go.

Distant Horizons

Beneath the sun, I lose my hat,
Running from the seagulls, imagine that!
With each wave, my laughter spills,
Chasing crabs with strange dance skills.

Beach ball bounces, into the sea,
I yell, "Come back, that's not for thee!"
Fish are grinning, shells in the sand,
They're holding signs that say, "Nice hand!"

Sunburns bloom, in shades of red,
I look like a lobster, it's time for bed.
Seashells gossip, waves make noise,
Even the wind plays with the boys.

So when you find a turtle's shell,
Don't think it served a time in jail.
Just craft a story, wild and bright,
And share it under the stars at night.

The Quiet Coastline

Waves whisper secrets, so soft and sly,
A crab photobombs me, oh me, oh my!
Sandy toes and salty sips,
I dropped my sandwich, what a trip!

A seagull steals my last potato chip,
I chase it down, now that's a flip!
My friends are laughing, rolling 'round,
While I'm wrestling with a snack thief bound.

Buckets spill, and sandcastles fall,
They're more like ruins, not grand at all.
We dig for treasure, or at least for fun,
In our own world, we're never done.

But as the tide pulls our castles away,
I guard my fries like they might sway!
With giggles echoing under the sun,
We find joy in chaos, oh what a run!

Tides of Time

The clock ticks slow by the shore today,
Where jellyfish dance in their jelly way.
I brought a kite, but it won't take flight,
Turns out it's stuck in a BBQ light!

A seagull squawks, it's quite the crooner,
Singing about my lost beach tuna.
With every wave, the humor rolls,
As I trip, the ocean swallows my goals.

Sunscreen squirts, a slippery delight,
I look like a greased pig, pure sight!
Laughter follows each little blunder,
As the surf composes its whimsical thunder.

With snacks gone missing and shoes that don't match,
I chase my flip-flops, what a catch!
In this foolish realm, laughter shines bright,
Every moment a poem, every mishap a delight!

Secrets in the Sand

Footprints lead to a buried surprise,
Or maybe a crab, just wearing a disguise!
With shovels in hand, we plot and we plan,
To uncover the secrets of our crafty clan.

I dig too deep, now I'm stuck to my waist,
My friends are laughing, oh, what a taste!
A wave comes crashing, my rescue on cue,
I shout, "Uh-oh! Now I'm in goo!"

Seashells whisper tales as we play,
In the sun-kissed afternoon sway.
Our laughter echoes, glistening bright,
As we build our kingdom, a comical sight.

So gather your wisdom from grains of the shore,
And let the beach teach you how to explore.
In every wave, a giggle can land,
As we share our secrets, hidden in sand.